In Defense of Puppets

—/\\~

Anthony DiMatteo

FUTURECYCLE PRESS

www.futurecycle.org

Library of Congress Control Number: 2015956088

Published by FutureCycle Press
Lexington, Kentucky, USA

ISBN 978-1-938853-95-1

In memory of Marion Louise DiMatteo

Contents

IV

V

Acknowledgments

I

Phoning the Dead

Voices of the dead taped
on my phone speak a metallic
residue of soul. Again and again
I linger over his "please leave me
a message" or her "what's cooking?"

I feel the whole person lurch back
from his slurring of an s or the rising up
of hello, standing in front of me with warm
hands, the living voice in an instant
all that I love of the other, jolt
to the chest reopening a wound.

This banal recording that mocks the idea
of last words, yet so sweet to my ears,
is this the soul? This slipping off the tongue
of the lost breath of another, is this
a passage into another world?

Thumb press of a mind that has
flown off forever, you wring a sponge
in the endless well I fill for you.

Chain-Reaction

Even the cat noticed, the guffaw
the baby loosed, grinning in delight,
so tickled with himself and the Queen,
smittened by her majesty, her golden hair,
one of her subjects by instinct the way
a lion won't hurt royalty in fairyland.
He pulls the sovereign to his mouth,
but whose hand squirms in whose sleeve?
He makes me marvel at his wonder,
joy of laughter without words, first
alert to the cosmic joke of life,
alive despite all odds, like a puppet
and not like one, king without country,
little master ruling over our world.

In the Book of Numbers

What is it to listen to one breathe
among many strangers, to see oneself
as another or a cloud or doorway?
I like my numbness as a number.
I rest assured I am a fact, a stat,
admiring the light illuminating us,
my fellow breathers. Sign flashes my name
but I am not the person they say I am.
They say I have the wrong birthdate
as if someone should have told my mother.
I have to reapply, born five days later
than the official record where some
sleepy clerk put down a three for an eight,
twin circles of infinity left open.

I once was fifty short of being drafted,
birthdays announced over the speaker
in a college cafeteria. We young men
sat praying with our heads down.
Two were claimed from among friends,
off to Vietnam within three months.
One came home six months later
with only one leg. Figures never lie,
adding up by themselves to forever.
If we don't mess up or make them up,
they measure what is but turn us all
from a who to a what, heads in a row
while somewhere a baby falls into time
out of the universe without end.

A Maying on the Operating Table

My body looks up at me from my toes sometimes as if to say, "What the frig are you doing up there? You think words are a path? Try down here. Catch my view, the sidewalk vistas of small change and empty butts, the ants running for shelter in the shift of your tight shoes. Floor turns field turns street turns park. You notice me only when something stubs."

Here on the chiropractor's table, face down, typing into my phone, I have to respect my toe's warning along with my back's—although I never see my back the way I can my feet, knees, prick, belly, arms and hands. Hello knees—sorry for the extra work lately but the back's out on leave. I hear the doctor's assistant call out the name "Corinna," and the name alone makes me think of moon-shaped eyes, glistening streams, sleepy shepherds and whether or not she has gathered up the roses yet. Hurry up while ye may, O fairest of the feast!

But when the sweet haze of electric stim is over, the doctor flips me like a flounder and puts his weight on me. My ages-old soul flaps over green fields and centuries to smack into a little room of pain as my stubborn spine almost clicks into place. Green-gowned Corinna turns into smoke when I hear the gray-haired secretary say, "Come in here," to the next hunch-backed shepherd. Still, I can feel down to my toes an itch to nibble the grass again. I wink down at them, letting them know I'm up here, headstrong for life and for whatever flowers may come our lurching way.

Thank you, O universe, for this body brewed for millennia gliding before us like countless stars and sheep.

Six-word Stories

(after Ernest Hemingway)

Car left running,
two drinks poured.

The dog's head tilts,
empty hall.

Over a wall, laughter
cut short.

The right pajamas,
the wrong occasion.

Would the sunrise
make them frantic?

The woods were blooming.
Who knew?

"Where's your clothes?"
the policeman asks.

Her face appears
in his drink.

One brave woman
hums a song.

A lost key turns
his mind.

In the drawer,
the ring waits.

Only the wolf's cage
stays open.

The Notch

(White Mountains, New Hampshire)

I've walked a long way to get this view.
It's how I imagine the country
two hundred years ago, most of it, anyway.
I've been out here before. When my feelings
begin to yellow like old photographs,
it's time to go back to the woods,
novocaine for the soul, as I think
in flip moments, waiting to pay a toll
or lost at a party where dead family members
roam, dreaming of a moose
standing in a misting pond. I know
a view is not a thing or a drug,
and the name for the place the Notch
names more the feeling of being there
than the site. But that such has a name
misleads. More than a chipping away
with the wind for an axe is at stake.
The Notch is more stitch than cut, less path
than way, more what does without words
than what craves them, more what frees
than what pulls strings. What if
one's walking a road so early in the morning
it's not yet morning though birds are
stretching their wings? Or better yet,
poised in the middle of the Sound that cliff-
like time of day when darkness waits
for light and the waters are not flat
but restive, having rowed out to where
a sandbar is about to disappear and
the silence of the earth is apparent?

Yes, what if one is floating there,
beginning to realize the immensity
of a moment when time and space have yet
to divide into what we call a place,
when some hand taps on the shoulder
and one wakes in a parking lot or doctor's chair?
Yes, to stand once in the Notch
is to dream it ever, to shrink, to enlarge.
It's contrary but even more like being
on both sides of a mirror or falling
down while looking up or being held up
by the sky while looking down into it
from beneath a crisscross of pine.
Or having fallen out of love, one feels
first dawn the enormity of its loss.
Standing there is to look back at the one
outpost of humanity that looks like
the one outcrop of rock to be seen for miles
in that singular way through many mountains
not yet cut by highway or lines. Behold
the Notch where the heavens have not
been cleaved from earth and the din
and dust of human engines have almost
been erased like the scree of mighty rock
cascading down and the falls beyond named
after a man, Thoreau, who never stepped foot there,
how all begins and slips from the stones
that would hem them in. Being
there, one seems to fathom the before
and after of the whole race of man,
both the entering and breaking
of a dream and the silence
once spilled forever ringing out
in every room and field, even inside
one's mouth or cupped between one's hands.

Afterlives

It's a bad time for home and country.
A war goes on everywhere and nowhere.
I'm thumbing through a rare facsimile
copy of Americana in the form of a blue
notebook Whitman kept, whose hope
near guttered out during the Civil War.
It was his gift to us, given me by my first wife,
two dusty blue volumes in a blue case.
Hand of fate drops out from one
in the form of a photograph taken of me
by a stranger on a *traghetto* to Capri.
Petting a dog that looks just like our dog,
I wear the ribbed T-shirt I wore to bed
last night, not worn in fifteen years since.
My left hand in the picture and life
is scraped below the index finger.
Cut by coincidence or stroke of fate?
I think of loved ones no longer here,
and though I know any ghost
mimics me, it's as if a curtain
flutters or a book opens and some
voice tells me to laugh and forgive,
to feel the wild joy the universe makes
in the form of a wake as it passes
by us, into and out of our lives.

Second Nature

The dead have had it, tired of being
used for rhetorical effects—the wind,
the dark, the silence. It's not cold out there
for them, and gestures through smoky windows
look ridiculous through the trees that appear
to be on fire with the lamps of the New Year.
They look in at the shadows we'd have them be,
disappointed that we feel so melancholic over them.
It's tough in the state of annihilation but the living
have it much harder, trying to train themselves
to dance on air. Forget it. It'll be second nature.
The music will be so perfect no one will hear.

Things I Wouldn't Say to My Mother

Anything goes—almost—with her.
"I'm ordering the piss clams," she'd finger to me,
instead of "*linguine con vongole, per favore,*"
reserved for the waiter. She thrice predicted

when someone would have a baby,
knowing it was a boy or girl too as if
she had a part-time job as a sibyl
no one knew. She'd ask first thing,

"what's cooking?" because she knew
something always stirred the broth
of my busy brain. She was right.
Don't say "not much" or "nothing really."

That kind of nothing that sets up walls
was intolerable. "Get off it, come on,
ream it out for Christ's sake."
The day before she died she had a tough time

getting on her bra so I had to leave the room,
and my sister asked her why bother with it
as she struggled to work it on in her sick bed.
"You want me to die with my coconuts hanging out

like some passed-out floozy or something?"
I cracked up in the foyer, then sobbed.
"You alright out there? Something wrong?"
That was classic Mom. But once she let

her guard down a week before she died.
When I walked into her independent room,
she turned away her tears. "Let it out,"
I said. "Give them to me."

"It's not death I fear," she said, looking
into my eyes. "It's leaving my six behind.
I want to know how things turn out for you."
Even in her death, she thought of life.

And now as stars fade in or out,
turning the seasons but always marked
in points of light against an infinite dark,
I think I know how to die.

Release

She pours whatever comes out,
instrument of her instrument, rest
and pulse of fingers on the keys,
scales for five digits out of Liszt,
the way birds skim the tips of waves.

She'll soon join Bach ahead, freed
from his score as if she were he,
altering his route but facing the same
mountain. Stairs are hewn by her stream,
whirling the way over hammered shards.

On the summit a crown of sun awaits
where birds rest on a teetering edge
facing one way until the final moment

silence flies out from uplifted hands.

II

Home Visits

He wants to go home to his mother
whose blood I see has poured
on the couch. ID in hand, I've opened
her door to find her out of her mind.
I'll file my report, but what to say to her boy?

Another child hopes to return to the one
bucket, the one table and the one bedroom
where three siblings slept on 123rd Street.
Waiting for a clanking elevator,
I get a hard stare in the lobby.
O stranger, is this our stranger land?
Three apartments share a bathroom
where part of the wall is missing.
One can see the East River from the toilet.

Another boy's father I interview
in the park where he lives. He asks
how I found him and says the child's
not his. The mother suffers from diabetes
and babysits six children: "This is
what sweet Jesus wants me to do."
Her twenty-year-old man-child appears,
grabbing my briefcase. He asks
if I have something sweet for him.

Most of the boys in our group home
long to go home, to the broken
family that issued them to the world.
I want to break down a wall
and rescue them, but in their eyes
I am the one cutting at strings.

Only Now

Must I go there again? The same stairs
not seen in years, the door opened by hands
I don't know? When I look away from stars,
I never doubt they'll be there again
without me. It's no matter of trust,
the way I don't trust the sun to rise
or blame the night for filling the sky.
Who speaks that way? But when I think of you,
I'm blind before a creaky gate, the alley
flooding with night where a wild rose cuts my hand.
Who buries emotions? Who holds a cloud?
But I am not fooling myself about love anymore.
There's no return; it's only given. There's only
now and if not, a shadow in our arms.

The Prophet

They say he traveled two thousand miles
just to remind us how silence sounds.
They say his voice was like wind in a desert,
random, sad and full of weight.

When face to face, he spellbound all within reach.
When his back was turned, who knew to laugh or cry?
Where he lived in the mountain, no one knew.
Where such a one would live, no one knew.

Those who follow him are merry as if drunk.
Those who deny him are angry even when drunk.
Those certain of his truths bask in the shadow.
Those doubting them go blind from the light.

This is the first of prophets to end a long line of them.
This is the last of prophets to shout the end of things.
This time will be named after his deeds.
The times must be forgotten, one of his creeds.

He says people will call him more than man.
He says he was happy just to forecast rain.
He says he lives when people speak well of him.
He says he dies when they kill in his name.

Prima Facie

Arraigned with a crowd in the white house
freshly built for the shiny traffic court,
I sit, reading Seamus Heaney's book
rescued from debris. The court officer
calls for quiet, but I have fallen
into silence—no little riot for me.

I look over a river the poet makes
unshaded but shadowed.
On the margin the sun slants away.
The page shimmers. Who'd think
one Judge Stern over such a scene
would decree? Yet there's his name

embossed upon a plaque in letters
black and thin as his Texan tie.
"January 8th, no check that, the fourth"
he dictates to his clerk in a floral
sweater framed by the glistening walls
of the great wooden bench smelling
from oil soap—or is that his cologne?

She duly alters the date while my other
day slips off to dance among shadows.
There are mangled names. "Jay Nine,"
he stammers proudly, or "Rue Soo"
riding the vowels down a river
of lost time into the record book
she makes, barely fighting off sleep.

The poet has me looking for the dead
where the clock reigns over the quick,
but we the living will do, this patience
before the law the mass of us exude,
looking above and past the light.

"One hundred dollars please," his honor
tells me, dead last to go,
my story heard but ignored,
the price on my head affixed.
"Unjust," I mumble and pay.

As I walk out into the ocean
of night, I feel the greater debt
to what has escaped of the day alive,
the dead not yet having made their claim.
And I am happy to be a little free.

In Defense of Puppets

They are as pure as any dream.
Who takes fault with the moon?
Or kicks a stone for being in the way?
But what of werewolves and lovers
who blame their change on the moon
and the rage that turns man into beast
never seen before in a cage?

They are the pure among us,
children who mimic our words
not yet knowing the meaning,
or forests and streams, mountains
and deserts that echo all before.
Who pretends to silence them?
Their secret has no word.

They are the pure beyond us,
the murdered and betrayed
knife or breech cannot reach,
innocent as leaves of their fall
or waves and wind in a storm.
Who blames a scarf for a scent?
What ant deserves the random step?

They are the pure whose loss
defiles the stainer. Their would-be
master cannot make them love
or sleight of hand make them wrong.
A tree snaps too tightly staked.
A beaten dog acts out its owner's rage.
A broken boy kills with his father's hand.

They are the pure in trust,
goat led to slaughter,

unborn waiting to be born,
beggar uplifted by a crumb,
lover whose neck must be bent.
Their blood spills without thought
the way rain appears to weep.

The Religion of Poets

Who do these words belong to? Do you
want them? Let's make them free of charge
though history has rattled all over them,
snoring or screaming inside each of them.
Remove their badge of dishonor
and throw it to the floor. Use them
to make love or a song, pick
a fight or a scab. Lift them
from their tomb. Let it creak
for all to hear: the stars don't look
down and send us dreams,
and priests savor the pleasure of prayer.
Is not childhood the golden age?
And heaven the best of days?
In the beginning of time, metaphor began
and that is all we need to know.
Also, the dead and living nimbly work together
in a department for the lost and found.
Many a man has drowned in a flotsam
of things though nothing of value
can be stolen. Who steals love or faith,
hope or patience? The owl waits
without appointment, and parted
lovers still meet to kiss in the secret
dark of their minds. Who hears
where hearts beat in the hush-hush?
And look there at the meaning of words
up at the altar—a stood-up bride?
Or has she stood us up even as we say
not "I do," but "I get it"? O the meaning
of life. Where has she drifted off to?
I've heard she lives among mannequins
coming alive when the light is right.

But then, once in hand, a machine, a ghost.
Nothing we love or buy stays in place.
We drift in a more or less visible tide.
Meaning's the tail of a trout we cannot hold.
Words are a ship or train we jump aboard
to make a somewhere of nowhere,
lovers and tourists, strangers and nomads.
Warning: the conductor has fled
and the analogy can't get to sleep.
One's last breath is not the last stop.
Words are a blue train—and why not
make it blue?—and it is endless
in its slow approach towards the white
mountains silhouetted between them.

The Republic of the Universe

How to speak for the earth—
the trees and animals, the sky?
No, the affairs of the world—
how to make a little universe
out of a mirror.

The boy flies a string kite above
the Mediterranean blue and green
of the Gaza Strip. What does
the beach know of its name?
The boy will come to know.
A car rattles up the hill
behind a man in white robes,
arms akimbo, watching the photographer
no doubt, carefully, the picture of his son

to fly above that of Tony Blair
addressing Congress, one arm,
the right one, rested, the left,
with all the fingers stretched out,
the mouth open in a seizure
of speech. "The Force of Reason
Will Win Out." Black letters unfurl
the headline like a banner caught

on electric wires. Let us not
confuse these neat columns for reality.
Let us not mistake reason and force.
The one-time prime minister looks away
from a dead girl below, "Twice Discarded,"
the cold wit of the headline reads,
making a Eurydice out of little
Stephanie, in birth and death, tossed out,
murdered twice in this our Iron Age.

Beneath her headstone, a man
looks for a golf ball, Tiger
Woods, lost beneath the brief account
on unfriendly White House mail.

Has a whole way been lost, a whole
belief in the family of mankind gone
still? And yet a kite can be flown
the way stones can drop and fingers unclench.
A different kind of search and seizure,
the terrors of love, the sorrow of loss,
may find us queuing up together
against a wall one day, waiting our turn
to weep tears beneath the sun
on the common ground of tree, sea, and sky
right there before our soggy eyes
on any front page of *The Daily* or *The Times*.

Holiday Song

Not every day do I
stumble over a stone
walk a dead friend home
sip some silence

count ripples on the sand
hail crow's feet on flesh
respect the turtle's pace
return a pebble to its stream

shun the fake and narrow
rest in a field of shadow
respect the tenacity of weeds
feel the bruise of the sun

piss on a pointed gun
or use a comma, check
false pride by listening
to the smallest of birds

face my greatest fear
look a snake in the eye
hear a bark break dream's fog
touch the light in a beggar's hand

relish the swaying of trees
walk off without a goal
heed the indifference of stars
consider what a river needs

cherish what I cannot reach
give with no hope of return
bring a lost dog home
live with the end in sight

forget what I have to do
know I can do the deed
trust when lost for words
listen without waiting to speak

close my eyes missing you
gaze deep before day's end
find the courage to forgive
praise the wonders of your soul.

No. Not every day's
a holiday
though any day
might be our last.

The River, the Sky

Paul Klee said he would work
so as not to cry But where do
tears go if not to the same root?

Compressing the sky
into a single bolt is hard work
even for the sky, much less

the artist rubbing a bow on the edge
of a sheet of tin covered with sand,
in the quaking puppetry of which

the whole of art consists, Klee
analogized. Yet if he drew
a lucky silence in, the river might

let him taste the sky in his hand.

The Truce

Ancient rift between sisters and brothers
kept us apart, and now he's here at my door,
first cousin not seen in fifty years or more,

three inches taller, year older than I,
and big moon eyes like my father had,
his own long since closed off from the sky.

No one of that generation is left alive,
but their feud has outlived their flesh.
Who knew hatred thrives beyond the grave?

Now we stand at a threshold and weep
like brothers made to fight a civil war.
He had looked me up, afraid to call

lest I suspect some prank or malice.
But I shudder from another dread.
Who will return in dream to open my eyes

upon no field of my own? No matter.
The dead call no truce. Only the living can.
Sharing first names, I embrace this man.

III

Recall

I am in the garden. You
are not. My memory
of you is in the garden.

The voice of a child
streams by in my head.

When I return to where I am,
I know love is not life.

Nothing ever stays green.
We love what we lose twice.

There's no other way.
Recall.

Race

We Cowboys line up in the dusty field,
tighten to command, a hand raised,
a whistle. Straining into manhood,
our bodies explode in the race, tensing,
releasing, lifting, letting go
at a distant flag. We make the end
rush towards us, reversal of drudgery
the schedule brings. We fix time
through sinews strapped to mind.

At race's end, victors emerge
clear as day. Two dark boys
we all knew would darken our day,
tasting their dust left behind, smirching
our egos, our two black heroes,
hope of the whole season,
on this field better than anyone white.

A "bull-line" forms in the reddened sky,
ten of us on each side, facing each other,
between them a matador to run,
charging straight ahead at his loving tackler,
their embrace but a fury of revenge
in this hard game from men. I cradle the ball,
stampeding low, hammering ahead
at my appointed foe, fleetest of boys.
I astonish him and me, an energy
boar-like that drives me over him
as he clings to my knees, perfect tackle,
though my thrust gains a yard of silt.

We both rise in dusty dreariness.
In his eyes, I see disappointment
with me. "How could you let them
work you so hard against me, friend?"
he seemed to say, and I felt ashamed,
red with the blood summoned by his gaze.

Power

Two boys, we'd sneak down to the pits
where your father kept his cool machines,
bulldozers and cranes. One day you promised
keys, and it coincided with the arrival
of our new bikes, week after Christmas
in the cold, dull light. We slipped off,
rode the wind like crows the two blocks
to where the ground had been ripped open.

No men roamed the twisted piles of rock
where the machines slept like dinosaurs.
We climbed the biggest one of them all,
nervous for you held the magic key.
"Here goes nothing," you said and cranked
the behemoth into life. It rumbled under us
and the land gave way. You lifted
the brake and off we went. I shivered
with fear, you with delight, as you raised
the huge bucket high in the air
and crashed it down and down again,
splitting boulders. I jumped out of the cab,
back to wait with the bikes. You plowed
along ridge after ridge, victorious.

Your father had all the money, I thought,
mine all the brain, and this was my destiny,
to watch the loud movers of the world
dominate. I gripped a quarter in my fist
and used it to slash the blue metallic paint
of your prized bike, which had so many more
gears than mine. My father would be proud,

I mused, finding the seam beneath my
treachery where I could hide, blaming
my act on fathers, how they score and scour
the earth. The coin burned in my hand.

When you came back, I looked down
to the dirt, redder than the sun
setting on my deed. "My bike, what did
you do to it," you asked, "why did you?"
I babbled only, "because I could."
That day we both left childhood
and friendship behind, learning how
to make sense of betrayal and regret
and the hard ways of men. For me,
a burning question began: what to do
with the small change left of my innocence.

Coincidence

The force of it staggers
as when lost in a forest
you return to the very spot
you start from. A moose
stands grazing by the flippant stream.

Then yesterday, visiting my mother
in the hospital, I saw our once upon a time
neighbor's name three rooms down the hall
just as she had lived three houses down
thirty-five years ago. The daughter

cried out my name, told me I looked
just like my father, then corrected herself,
no, my mother, and I stared in wonder
at how this woman still dressed as if
it were the seventies. "Remember

those pears?" she asked me, "how they
just happened to drop on my mother's side
of the fence, and we couldn't resist
though your grandmother howled through
our kitchen window, 'those are my pears'—

remember?" I couldn't but laughed as if
I did. My mother had to fill me in,
how her mother who lived next door
just happened to see the red pears
gleaming in the window. In high style,

she claimed her fruit, her custom
to wear a mink jacket just to walk
her terrier down the block. Imagine,
she could have bought ten orchards
of pears but those were hers

though branches pour down
her fence. The noon light
has to hit the six pears just right
or she never sees them—
but of all the stories to tell!

Surely this was not my elegant
grandmother's best moment.
"Must have been the ice cream
on the pears they served with dinner,
that's the trigger," my mother muses.

Later, as I enter the dark street,
I see the light in my mother's room
go out the same time as the one
three windows down, the kind of thing
I'd notice as a child but not since.

I could see again the lights flicker off
on that old tree-lined street one by one
until only a few stars remain
and a breeze out of the night
nudges a bough heavy with fruit.

Trouble in Paradise

(On Mantegna's Parnassus)

The universe spins with desire so the old
painter implied to the *marchesa.* Even war
is made to serve love in the long run,

the reason why only Venus conquers Mars.
Should he fall out of union with her,
madness would reign in a world he'd raze,

and the dance of the Muses would cease.
For a glorious moment, however,
Mantegna maintains a delicate balance.

Perhaps Isabelle appreciated only too well
the painter's vision that raised on high
the white goddess as gentle overlord.

But why peace from war at such a price?
And how to justify her infidelity
to Pallas on another wall storming vice?

O what to do with the adulterated god,
lame smithy of Olympus, Vulcan
madly fuming in his smoky cave? See

his anvil placed above the lyre of the poet
who too longs for what can be imagined
but not held. He gazes beyond the dance

towards a greater light of what could be
if only war would break its lance
and fretful husbands went to sleep.

Zoological

The road acts greater than the path
but one outwalks it, reaching a wood.
The path knows how to be undone,
offering lessons in solitude under leaves
whose open hands have flown to their fate
down through the air, no flight alike—
as if in semblance of many a road—
but their destination's the same. The end
is the last piece of the path to fall
into place. It is greater than the path.

Some think they have lost the way
should the road drift to a halt.
Parents may prove no friend,
for instance, the fate of so many
of the boys once under my care
in the group home. But then past
the shadows of woe that poured
down around them like leaves,
they found life greater
than those who engendered it.

One time we stood about in a zoo,
six boys and I watching pigs
whoop it up, two males in the pen
grunting round the female, one blocking
her way, the other mounting from behind.
And when the boar finished with the sow,
as he leaped off her, semen shot through
the air, falling on our shirts and hair.
We cried out, then laughed. "No escape,"
a boy said. "It comes down like rain."

Echo Chamber

In the vast echo chamber of the world
people try hard to be heard or remain silent,
afraid of dying or dying alone or being taken
for a fool or giving without receiving. We
clamor for originality but end up repeating
or being repeated without recognition.

What can't be echoed can't be verified
or traced back to the maker who's no owner.
Who owns a shadow or image?
Even one's clothes belong to something else
at one remove from what it once was.

I was surprised to find my heart
an echo chamber too, the dreams
and poems that cannot get arrhythmia,
a figurative pump, puppet and cleft.
"Follow your heart" is said
in many a song and street.
Catch up to the path cut by dream.

The mind imagines a bloodless heart
because it wants to be off the hook—
who follows one's heart to work harder?
It wants a rosy hearth outside the echo chamber
where everyone is a version of everyone else.
Some commit someone else's suicide,
love someone else's love or covet
another's life or talent or sneakers.

One thing is certain. No specter bleeds,
loves or dies. Try to pin it down

and it's an airless balloon, failed replica,
making it unique though derivative,
a copy without an original, indicating the way
we think about things is inadequate
in the vast echo chamber that is the mind.

Recognition

Trees ready for snow on Furman Lane,
throwback to the nineteenth century.
It's about density now, many mouths
to feed, from which words, from which noise.
London plane and maple have thinned out,
leaves escorted off in neat bags. Happiness

I've heard still occurs in uncollectible
ways: the night after the storm, that
moon, or the time you lost keys.
We swayed the boat more than
anyone knew, the laughter
and tears that defined us, long since

stolen off. O why does time
compare to a thief or a bird?
Some even say it marches.
I say a few yellow and red leaves
shiver in the morning sun on the lane
and never queue up to form a parade.

Walking over their ghosts on the way
to the supermarket, I hear the sheep
that perchance bleated under a stand
of beech, only one of which remains.
Elsewhere in the little city once
a sleepy village, in the quiet offices

of vendors and lawyers, developers
and bankers, white papers rest in neat
sleepy piles. Even blank they are never
empty. One can see the sun pass by
over their surfaces and over the skin
of busy people, and over the black

puddles black tires endlessly splash.
At the end of the lane, across from which
the bay is relieving itself in ripples,
I see a crow land and hop along.
It tilts its head when a cloud makes
a shadow fly as if it had thought

only a bird could. And now it knows.

IV

Outburst

Something of the most urgent matter
eludes us when we tell only the facts
of our lives the way in Kollwitz's *Outbreak*
features of individual figures are lost
to a blur of movement as we look deeper
into the picture, and yet how deeply each
of us believe in our lives, our uniqueness,
the worthiness of our cause. Consider
the impact of time on one's love or face,
how it shows us to be just another one
who laughed and cried, who in the mirror's
deepening lines of shadows traced
a sunset through a thicket of trees.
And yet how I love life. And you.

A Bequest and a Prayer

The pyramids would have the sun honor them,
my love, casting their blank shadows
when nearly all were slaves. Elsewhere,
heads with honey were filled and placed
on shelves in dovecote tombs. Now we walk
among endless graves etched with acid rain.

Each hour we meet those who will outlast us,
but that's no cause for alarm. Nor will there be
a way to steep our ghosts in their tea.
Among our cremators or inhumers, let us
take no offense and make merry.

The hands of others will burn or dress us.
Between fire and earth, one must choose.
Join sun motes to muck up the air
or check in solo into a windowless room.
Are there beds enough for all the dead?

Ashes to ashes in either case because it's not
about space but time. The future living,
my sweet, will be forced not to shelter
the next few billion to die lest megastorms
loose sleeping bodies to float down Main Street.

So incinerate me, my love, should you
outlive me, and I pray that you do,
for I would not burn from the longing
you would have left me to bury inside.
I would rather burn in death than in love.

And that is my bequest, this my prayer.

Workers of the World

All morning I've been occupied
trying to wake up sleepy metaphors.
Time flies. Hearts break. Suns rise.
I can hear the Latin music of workers
on the roof of the old house next door.
Two of them are on the top of its spire—
are they from Peru or Chile, so indifferent
to height? They talk about girls and wine.
At least that's what I imagine from the way
one holds his heart and sways. One can fall
in love as easily from a roof, but out of it?
It's like climbing a steeple with oily legs.
That's what I'd have him say, dragging him
into my poem without stopping him from work.
He's got a wife and kids and needs to get paid
by the fast-talking white dude who'll show up
in his big red truck later in the day
when the sun has started its fall from the sky.

Miscegenation

The biggest bang is the one no one's heard.
Purity of blood has nothing to do with type
just as race knows nothing of the person.
And shouldn't someone tell the cormorants
they don't belong in our neighborhood?
They sit on the rocks where river meets bay,
best view and seafood in town. Damn bird
pays no taxes and has the utter gall
to chase the native gulls away.
What's next? A state permit to feed?
I watch their little black heads bob up
amidst the stream, out of nowhere,
like the stars in these waters at night
seeping into dreams a wayward seed.

Anxious Axioms

Trust is an open cage.
When locked, there's only rage.

Love carries off—think kingfisher.
Love's on the brink—think fish.

Some people are naked while clothed.
Some people are clothed when naked.

The feet must take to dance
for the head to feel the trance.

Sooner fish without a string
than wear love like a ring.

Inside any master's plan
hides a child behind the man.

A tree reaches with its root.
A path's bigger than one's boot.

Hands must make the start
if one would follow the heart.

On the other hand there's
the other hand. Beware.

Elbows play a role
when one rests the soul.

Better to be love's fool
than treat a lover cruel.

No storm acts from malice.
Behind a smile may lie ice.

One must bow the head
for love to make its bed.

The Poem to the Poet

I sit outside your words.
You lure but must let go,
from the marble free,
a wave of the sea.

In wilderness I thrive, other
to the voice you give me.
You'll close the gate,
pleased with your captivity.

Before parsed, time and space
unfold as one, no border.
Who'd arrest stars for disorder,
chain a river, or hold wren

and wind responsible
for dancing with a branch?
I am the joy none relive
or, indifferently, trail of a tear.

My spark thrilling your song
creates your career. Hear me
in the woods before I am scored.
Why do you think me your gift?

So would a tomb bring security
or a place of birth identity,
signs of a fall into discord.
The field is greater than we see.

My greetings bode sadness,
angel of lost wings.

Once the flight's over,
I take them back.

Ride a rainbow or kiss
a star. Do you mistake
the moon for glass?
Does the sun rise and fall?

As soon as your foot falls,
I fly away. You shadow me
in a desert once paradise.
Follow me to enter it

but never stay.

Interior Survey

Have you ever wandered
outside your fish bowl?

Do you see others
snorkeling inside it?

Have you ever slept
on the shoulders of a mountain?

Have you ever seen a lion
weep in its cage?

Can you recognize the child
you left behind?

How often do you trust
your feet to find the path?

Are you happy only if
you don't think about it?

Are you sad
and don't know it?

Isn't ignorance in bliss
ignorant about bliss?

Are you longing to do
what you never will?

Are you longing to do again
what can be done only once?

Will you do one day
what you never imagined?

Can you see what your hands
have done in a mirror?

Can you see yourself seeing
yourself without a mirror?

Is your plan for life
the result of chance?

Is there any chance
you have not planned it out?

Do you love others
as other than yourself?

Are we versions of each other
in search of each other?

Can we feel the joy
that gives up hope?

Can we live together
in this dream of now?

Job Envy

I look up at the mountains out of blank time,
my blank time. There's the blackest rock
I've ever seen, foothold for a distant crown.
It's off the side of the road doing what it does.
Imagine being one is all I can do,
servant to a remote lord, for example.
But the mountain is neither
man, beast nor god. It does not have
the back I see turning away from my eyes
to fly off with a lovely cloud of its own making.
It's as if it needed a little privacy, caught naked,
like a snake or oligarch in recoil from public view,
yet ruling over a world it has no pretensions
to defend or own, its occupation
to occupy only itself.

O Mary Lou

Midsummer Mary Lou's getting hauled
across the way, surrounded by the sweaty men
of Weeks Marina. She sways gently in the lift.

Elsewhere, perhaps the Mary Lou
the ship's named for walks the halls
of a nursing home to greet the dim light.

And somewhere else still another
Mary Lou might fidget with a pile of bills,
pouring herself a second bolt of gold

crisp with the light of this morning's air
that also makes clear not all Mary Lous
are imaginary, just as all those songs

must have been about someone real
easy to greet and hard to say goodbye to.
Who'd believe such passion can be sung

to a cipher? But one never knows—
no slur against Ricky Nelson here
or Dante or Petrarch whose woman

of the light neither could hold as wife.
Who'd complain of longing when
one could linger on for toast in bed?

And all those boats named for women
may not be named after one on land.
Still, across the river, there can be no doubt

men are hard at work on the Mary Lou.
High aloft she swings in twin belts of steel,
hanging and creaking like the trees that made her.

"The canvas is never empty"

—Robert Rauschenberg

Because the brain needs a wheel.
Because the light pours in silence.
Because the future casts a shadow.
Because a man drowns at a table.
Because a woman refuses to model.
Because memory is a wet dog.
Because of the majesty of the moment.
Because a dream swatted a fly.
Because people walk around hungry.
Because of what the painter steals.
Because the poet gets the last word.
Because of my fear of loving you.

v

Puppets

"The people moves as one spirit"
—Geoffrey Hill, "De Jure Belli et Pacis"

Most of the boys in the home believed
themselves puppets. Their parents
junkies and whores, deadbeats and thieves,
what could they do but repeat their fate?
I heard this story so often I'd fall asleep
with eyes open, instrument myself
of powers I could not rise above.
It was all a pretense, a mask speaking
someone else's voice the way a vision
takes over the mind needing to dream.
Need. Want. Who chooses feelings?
But only the first moves with strings
jerking us around, housed in bodies
as we are. Want is what we believe.

The Sisters

One time two sisters share a train,
admiring each other's Christmas scarf
among a New York press of strangers—
as if time or place has anything to do
with our bodies whose histories are painted
with the big brush of the universe,
itself never one verse and thus misnamed,
sleepy metaphor, with hairpins on and
eyes closed beneath the ownerless stars.

Through swaying heads, the two
catch sight of a figure they know—
blue eyes, dirty blonde hair beneath a veil—
could it be as if in dream their sister
not seen for years, born between them
nearly sixty years ago? (Silly to count
when one is headed towards infinity.)
Yes, there she is though seen so long ago
they fear they're seeing a ghost.

The three hug each other and laugh,
can't believe what randomness has wrought,
the childhood they had and lost,
knowing each other down to the scent,
to beauty marks and hidden scars.
After she departs, the two wonder if
they'll ever see her again though sure
they'll go to each other's funeral.
They saw that bond in each other's eyes.

Two Brothers

You left me there despite my plea,
lost in a spruce hole though later
I exaggerated how deep.
How you cheered to see me
when I stumbled out of the wild
hours after you'd arrived at the lean-to.

"Man can die in one of those traps,"
a ranger told us the next day.
"Wasn't for that whistle, officer Jack
would've died. Did you blow yours?"

I hadn't one, had to crawl and scrape
my way up, first my pack, then me,
difficult climb from hell, then free.
I was stunned when you said, yes,
you had heard me shout your name.
And still you left me there, lost
off trail, ten feet down an icy slit.

Just where one thinks a little bush,
hole in the ground, tree growing sideways,
hiding a drop six feet or more.
A man falls quick as an anvil
through rotted wood in a floor.

Some of what we had between us
that day blew away into dust.
I have tried hard to forget it.
And I admitted to you my lie.
It took me a half hour to get out,
not one, and the bruise from a spill
came later on, down some slick rocks.
I've caught my own colds
from the devil's mouth.

I forgave you your cruelty,
accepting your apology.
But the truth was you left me there.
You cared only for your rage.

And now the call has come to claim you.
You've been murdered, my brother.
How unspeakably sad.
Our sister and I cried when we saw
you stretched out inside death's bag,
your face frozen with disbelief
from what a friend turned killer
was willing to do, stabbing you
with your own kitchen knife.

Hunger for beauty, what drove us
up the mountain, could not outstep
this anger of man against men.

Still, we need not track the open
field ahead with a trail
we'd leave behind. And the way
up sometimes first does go down.
This is what I need to believe
despite a pessimistic view of man
frozen into place for centuries.
If it were man against man in a state
of nature, we'd all have disappeared.

What kindness out of loss might it be
for us now if not for us then as kin?
Had I not fallen, I'd have never seen
the beaver down Mount Marcy, working
the Hudson's source, Lake Tear of the Cloud,
name of an ancient tarn as well as
of the wound between us then
and the grief I feel now.

I sat there watching him build
as the moon rose and I drank.
Maker of a river greater than any
he could know, he tolerated me
in his work as I thanked my fate.

That was the astonishment on my face
when we met at the lean-to that night
in the absolute dark, my brother.
I had just sat with a god
of the Adirondacks and drank
from his star-filled stream.

What of the anger between men
to him and to the gift of this
vision that has remained?
And now, I live for two, you
in the wind, and me on the ground.

Grand Concourse

(Bronx, New York)

The street swirls with cars and litter now,
the stores largely the same, although
Alexander's has long gone with its
low-priced imitations of designer clothes.
But I don't know where I am, feeling lost
and white in a place that once felt like home.
This is not to say it is not exciting
to be among black and Latino faces
like white-out in a sea of ink. Memories
seep in, sinking my step, slowing my
hands across the shut metal gate
of the Loew's Paradise Theatre. The high
décor inside gathers dust and webs now,
blotted out fingerprints on brass rails,
red velvet seats still pressed
by ghosts who sit there watching
John Wayne, James Bond and Jaws.
My mother and I had seen the last film
side by side, her nails digging into my arm
when the shark bit the man in two.
It was a big deal, going to the movies then,
so much so I was not allowed to go
alone with friends. Now the dead sit in rows
all dressed up before a blank screen.
When the money left, the theater shut up too,
leaving behind these stores to suck the poor dry,
chasing the illusions the rich like to buy.
Outside a pawn shop, I watch a couple
nervously kiss, hoping no one will see.
My parents had married a half century ago
at the Grand Concourse Plaza Hotel
where now a man on a megaphone invokes
God down upon the sinful masses: O padre Dio!

I drift towards distant trumpets burning
above conga drums in a puddle of rotting food
I am standing in, holding my broken camera,
catching gazes of the people glancing past me,
my pinkish skin and blondish graying hair
like a balloon floating above a white
dress shirt given to me one Father's Day.
Zoning out in recollection, I did not know
I had cut a line at a bus stop until someone
called out, "Dude, the end's back there."
I like falling in behind everyone else
though I was waiting for a bus I would not take,
pressed against the window of a store where
half-priced electronics long for suppliant hands.
A different lifetime was walking the streets
in my mind, and I too would disappear.
Paradise would reopen and seal up again,
and all the races of the world would imagine
who they once were but no longer are,
as we stand there in the future trying
to recall the people we did not see
even when we were here, lost in the flesh.

Black Day

(April 20, 1989)

For me, that Thursday, the hundredth
anniversary of Hitler's birth, proved
blacker than any night I had known.
It was the day after the Central Park jogger
was left for dead, the alleged black males
no more than a bunch of boys. My sister
about to graduate from a Catholic college
wanted them hanged even after their ages
were disclosed. She made this big gesture.

I could not control my tongue, broke
the silence of a parliament of heads
nodding in agreement. "But they're
only wild kids maybe and you want
strange fruit in the park? Is this
the fruit of your education?" I asked.
"How dare you..." she said. Our father stood up.

"So if they had raped your sister
You'd— what?—let them live
there in the group home with you, right?
What kind of a man are you?
You're my fruitcake for a son."
My mother tried to calm my father
and brother down. "Please go now,"
she said to me, "let's not have trouble."

"Have a nice day, everyone,"
I said, not quite at the top
of my lungs. On the drive home,
I lost the road when the moon
rose bravely in the night.

How little the void between stars
when compared to glaring space
between thoughts, the inky luster
of a pool where souls are drowned,
where a garden of death takes root
and a tree offers its blackening fruit.

My car veered onto the shoulder,
slipping down a bank of fatal thoughts
and their highways, their myriad
branches that shadow us together,
hang us down from the sky,
white, then gray clouds turning black.

If there is such a thing as the root
of evil I'd have to spit it out
of my own mouth. I'd have
to hunt down the very taste of it
in everything I eat, the scent of it
in everyone I love. Do I have
the strength to resist the sleekness
of its alluring crush upon
my palette, at the very table
where I break bread, the flowers
of its wiliness, words that cook life
in the slow simmer of a blind sun?

Forgive us, O sun of the morning,
should we forget to bless your daily race
different in kind from our rat race.
Keep us from despair,
benighted by the love of it.
Your light makes all mankind shimmer
though we hide behind a skin
made of mind you cannot burn.

Elegy for Heritage

Speak of birth dates
and nations? There's no place
or number, only the now,

families without borders,
citizens of the universe
cast into the light.

Which of us dreams up
what's ahead?
Puppets wait for hands.

Mother's a soft stone,
Father a giant, fitted out
to serve man, sovereign

and beast, a world at stake.
Toy soldiers and dolls collude.
We come to learn a role,

drone, pawn, clown or clone.
More than clocks are wound.
Mother smothers. Father bothers.

Home turns someone's house.
He'd preach, "I who gave you life
can take it back," old Roman code

that's outlasted even Rome
and why people say history's
a march and not a dance. Alas.

Mother held us together
and Father kept us down.
When he left the house,

we'd all come up for air,
drowning at his supper table,
strung out upon his words.

Master strikes without hands
(though he's too the marionette
no child thinks a father yet).

At the head of the stairs
hung the Cross as if
to say, "Expect no more

who pass this way."
No wonder we came of age
amidst divorces and rage

in nests of our own
tied down by strings
no one would own.

I think of soldiers of his day,
scripted for strife and
turned larval while alive,

taught war brings peace.
But more than ghosts
are on the hook. The cloth

trembles with life.
Voices stir the mask.
In dreams spills blood.

And now the horrible word:
my brother's been killed
in his own home.

At least not by his own hand.
The murderer's named Adam,
I read in the paper,

take-off from holy fable
or sick fairy tale. I thank
the God of Cain my mother's

not alive to feel more pain
from man set against man
in the maze of hate.

The artist in my mom
wanted out. She'd run
through rain to make us laugh.

Who knew her price paid,
her heart in it just for us?
The grand house we once had,

O what of that? Stage or trap
whose walls still flash.
Shadows dance in step.

Who asks to be born?
The root of childhood
leads to where one lives,

growing in an innocent country
of its own estate.
The majesty of the moment

flashes in a pigeon's wings
as it crowns the marbled great
who guard fountains of their name.

What child chooses a name
or loves not the water's splash?
What do rivers or mountains know

of borders claimed by states
in the name of God or fate?
Now crocus sprouts

of its own accord
and in woods burns
a line of green.

Spring makes me think
how my mother taught us
to love life more than suffer it,

her glorious heritage
left for others to heed.
She needs no house now.

The stars find her home,
those flowers of night
in nobody's garden, free.

Seeking Leonardo

Look at the light and consider its beauty—blink your eye and look at it again: what you see was not there at first, and what was there is no more. Who is it who makes it anew if the maker dies continually?
                                    —Leonardo da Vinci

Eyes like rain never arc the same way twice.
O Maestro, is this what you have in mind?
Prospettiva de' perdimenti, a prospect
of losses, sight losing sight of itself,
the closer things are, the less we see
how a distance looks back at us?
Space curves in time that has no
before or after though we look both ways.
The squirrel's acrobatics on a line
and a car turning while a ball hangs
on a rim spin out a synchronous destiny
with a bullet firing thousands of miles away
—who dies in Asmar?—all seizures
of the now pointed to, observed, buffered
by modes of reproduction making
a shadow dance before our eyes
as if we were our own *fantoccini.*
This, I think, is only partly what you mean.
The endless previews of loss and the trail
of beauty taking its sinuous course
through mountain vale and mane,
tree and smile, zygomatics
of the pure moment, are these not
a warning to overlords, your mirrors
of a higher justice? Swords and cannons
of your own design were in vain
in the face of such melancholic joy—
and which joy is not to be true?—
the kind your madonnas for a moment
share, the way in the juniper

Ginevra's hair disappears or how
La Gioconda hides the sanctity
of her tears. The holiness of the now,
bead work of the changing eternal,
pen, brush, song or mathematics work
into the languish of a golden shadow,
pixels amidst cinder. The work goes on
though none speak past the grave.
Your impenetrable closet of a life
has locked in others too who made notes
on the bright fields of the apophatic,
be it Dionysius, Rothko or Proust.
Catching a dream in flight from itself
down the vacuumed rooms of memory,
Leonardo, you'd laugh, if I may presume,
at the price our analysts charge
to do such work. For yours, kings,
dukes and sultans let you linger
in their gardens to amuse their mistresses.
You'd be sovereign in a better world.
You painted rainbows and mountains as if
an angel's wings had passed over them
although too small to lift the angel itself
just as the gleaming forest of your mind,
moti dell'animo, was dark with a matter
you could not transform. Any maker
is rear-ended by her own perceptions,
you imply. You joked how a man
stands in the place of his own erasure,
proud to fly his flag, lord of his hole.
Your wit unfurls a secret smile
on the passing away of all that exists,
your Last Supper like the finest
of wines spilled into the dust.
This is a blessing we are not
heir to and of the purest kind.

Candle and Book

Your mind and my world—
words spinning a darkness
that disappears in your sight.
No other way to hear them
except in silence, the leaves
not stirring but for the wind.
My eyes want to see
how you shine in the night.
Shadows flee your step,
a flock of black birds.
The wisdom you bring
is the beauty I seek.
Candle and book—
my world in your light.

Motives

Mockingbird cruises in to sing atop
my chimney's grill, triumphant.
"You will always be a failure
in your eyes. Not I. Not I."

Does he make windows into souls?
Why do I ventriloquize his song?
Orioles, wrens, starlings, blackbirds,
all rivals for his kingdom—be warned.

That must be the motive for his outbreak.
It's not mine. As he falls silent,
I slip into a pit of doubt.
You've entered the garden unaware

of how flowers mimic your hair,
driving me off to this page, to let fly.

Food

Eating with the muse, I forget to eat,
cooing the morsels of light on her lips
that curve the way wings do in air.
At best, a mist has already risen
between us; at other times, dense fog.
She enables my fictions, herself not
one of them. She stands outside my mind.
I yearn for traces of whatever food
her milk-laden mouth has left behind.
The crumbs of things speak to me clearly.
That is her power in me that uplifts me
out of myself. The words begin to tumble.
A blade of grass, some spilled water
on a broken table, reflections in ice
made by a tilted branch against the moon,
the dancing stream of desire in your eyes—
how the gold loves the soft dark brown there!
All these are intimations of her nature.
Feed the mind, leave the flesh.
Consume not what inspires you.
I gather the crumbs from the table
and fling them to the birds.

Still

I am still learning how to live
to the end. To keep it in sight,
one must see without eyes.

You say you don't fear death
and ask as if full of hope:
who feels anything when dead?

The sadness in your voice
your laughter cannot hide.
Silence fills a soft rain

falling between us. Which bead
alike in the driven gray?
Whatever is, has one path.

I think of a pyramid,
stone gateway for the soul
light as a feather

or a secret vow of lovers
made with one eye closed,
soul mates turned to ash.

I want to tell you
the sun is a rose.
Light is its scent.

If I groom the dog,
the day is good.
Tufts fall like petals

to become threadwork
for a nest. I follow
one drift to where a snail

has climbed high up
a sun-baked wall. So long
the way, so quick the fall.

I am still learning nothing lasts,
the world that we know
illusion in a cloud.

What of love in view of death?
Melodrama among talking beasts?
Who would deny it to the birds,

the giddy calls pouring down
from the trees each day,
the squabbles, the songs?

Can I ask about the sadness
in your voice? Is your life
a burden or a blessing?

Looking into your eyes,
I forget the terms of the question
but not why I am still here

climbing slowly up a mountain,
surrendering to you
without condition or knowledge

of what the end might be.

Acknowledgments

The author thanks the editors of the following journals for publishing poems from this book:

2 Bridges Review: "In Defense of Puppets"
The Cortland Review: "Second Nature"
Extract(s)—Daily Dose of Lit: "The River, the Sky"
The Inflectionist Review: "The Canvas Is Never Empty"
Long Island Quarterly (25th year anniversary issue): "In the Book of Numbers"
Waccamaw: "O Mary Lou"

Cover collage, "Ostrava Angel," from A Czech Dream Book Series (2008) by Marie Pavlicek-Wehrli; author photo by Kathleen O'Sullivan; cover and interior book design by Diane Kistner; Droid Serif text with Comic Sans titling

About FutureCycle Press

FutureCycle Press is dedicated to publishing lasting English-language poetry books, chapbooks, and anthologies in both print-on-demand and ebook formats. Founded in 2007 by independent editor/publishers and partners Diane Kistner and Robert S. King, the press incorporated as a nonprofit in 2012. A number of our editors are distinguished poets and writers in their own right, and we have been actively involved in the small press movement going back to the early seventies.

The FutureCycle Poetry Book Prize and honorarium is awarded annually for the best full-length volume of poetry we publish in a calendar year. Introduced in 2013, our Good Works projects are anthologies devoted to issues of universal significance, with all proceeds donated to a related worthy cause. Our Selected Poems series highlights contemporary poets with a substantial body of work to their credit; with this series we strive to resurrect work that has had limited distribution and is now out of print.

We are dedicated to giving all of the authors we publish the care their work deserves, making our catalog of titles the most diverse and distinguished it can be, and paying forward any earnings to fund more great books.

We've learned a few things about independent publishing over the years. We've also evolved a unique, resilient publishing model that allows us to focus mainly on vetting and preserving for posterity the most books of exceptional quality without becoming overwhelmed with bookkeeping and mailing, fundraising activities, or taxing editorial and production "bubbles." To find out more about what we are doing, come see us at www.futurecycle.org.

The FutureCycle Poetry Book Prize

All full-length volumes of poetry published by FutureCycle Press in a given calendar year are considered for the annual FutureCycle Poetry Book Prize. This allows us to consider each submission on its own merits, outside of the context of a contest. Too, the judges see the finished book, which will have benefitted from the beautiful book design and strong editorial gloss we are famous for.

The book ranked the best in judging is announced as the prize-winner in the subsequent year. There is no fixed monetary award; instead, the winning poet receives an honorarium of 20% of the total net royalties from all poetry books and chapbooks the press sold online in the year the winning book was published. The winner is also accorded the honor of being on the panel of judges for the next year's competition; all judges receive copies of all contending books to keep for their personal library.